The Restoration of Mut Neter

By Tanehesi The Restorer

©SameTreeDifferent Branch Publishing

Same Tree Different Branch Publishing

Copyright 2022 by Kofi Piesie Research Team

All right reserved. No part of this book may be reproduced or transmitted in any form or by any means, electronic or mechanical, including photocopying, recording, or by any information storage and retrieval systems without the written permission of the publisher.

Printed in the United States of America

Table of Contents

Dedicated

Chapter I - Introduction

Chapter II - But who is the Caucasian

Chapter III - The End of an Age

Chapter IV - The Importance of Education

Bibliography

DEDICATION

This book is dedicated to Iya, my arakunrin Chris, my omo Tedros, my immediate ebi (Isaiah, Saba, Rahel, and iyawo Zebib), and extended awon ebi like Garfield Reid, Ankh West, Kofi Piesie, Ini-Herit Shawn Khalfani and the Mossi Warrior Clan, the Dagger Squad, Pseudo Killas, Science with Shawn, SaRa Suten Seti, Sheena Lynne, Kecia Jones, Thurston Hargrove, John Pitts and all my supporters on social media as well as all of those who seek truth, wisdom, and understanding……… Remember that…….Tomorrow……..is not a given……..but yesterday was…….and today…..is being given………..

Those AfRaKaNs who walked the plank
Oh, how I remember that day
When those AfRaKaNs walked the plank
Oh, how I remember Goree
When those AfRaKaNs walked the plank
So many drowned in the Great Ocean
Are those AfRaKaNs who walked the plank
So many kept their devotion
Are those AfRaKaNs who walked the plank
Now many live in the States
as those AfRaKaNs who walked the plank
Must never make a mistake and forget
Those AfRaKans who walked the plank

CHAPTER I INTRODUCTION

CHAPTER I: INTRODUCTION

Since my youth, I've always loved my ebi and have honored the love and wisdom of Iya/Mut Neter and Nna/It Neter. They bestowed on me the best guidance ever when I asked them who was my Eleda. My Obi always advised me to honor those who walked before me and defend my Ebi. So in many ways, this could have been released as the first volume of the Book of Iya series. Still, I thought it was necessary to outline the methodological approach used to guide my perspective first just in case I could not continue writing due to various health issues.

However, given that I can still be productive, it is essential to develop the methodology needed to further elaborate on the fundamental principles outlining the paradigm. For many, this may present significant challenges due to the history of colonialism and the impact it has had on civilization. Nevertheless, it is critical to further expound on the development of Eurocentrism and expand it so that it may also include an analysis of Caucasians, in general, to understand the fundamental aspects of its imperialistic tendencies so that we may genuinely liberate colonized and oppressed people, especially those of AfRaKaN descent.

It is also essential to construct a working definition of what is meant by Existential Imperialism, which holds up to scholastic criticism from peers. Furthermore, although our description may be imperfect, it should open doors or make room for refinement by other AfRAKaN scholars and intellectuals primarily. When I read Paulo Freire's excellent book Pedagogy of the Oppressed as an undergraduate, not only did it open doors in my sense of consciousness as a young intellectual, but it also introduced me to the fundamental principles of liberation theology and methodology.

At the time, I didn't realize how robust this understanding was until I began to study more and read other great thinkers like Walter Rodney, Dr. Yosef Ben Yochanon, Dr. John Henrik Clarke, and Oluko Molefi Asante. But still, I was left with a natural conception of methodology until I discovered Oluko Molefi Asante's great work The Afrocentric idea. This work set the foundation for a genuinely AfRaKan centered methodology that would allow the recovery and restoration of all things AfRaKaN and use the AfRAcentric idea as a core element for research and analysis in our attempt to restore the traditional AfRAKaN perspectives.

After being introduced to the idea, I began to do more research. I read more, which allowed me to look at the history of existence from an utterly AfRAKaN perspective regarding AfRaKaNs, and the people are correctly known as Caucasians. Their viewpoint of AfRaKaNs and this reality we exist in itself.

CHAPTER II: But who is the Caucasian?

CHAPTER II: BUT WHO IS THE CAUCASIAN?

But who is the Caucasian?

First, it's essential to have a clear understanding of what we mean by the term "Caucasian." The following definition and map allow us to come to a good reference point to define what is meant in clear terms. The subject has been called white, European, and other names, but historically the truth is Caucasian is also correctly known as an Asiatic. So to this extent, you have an Asiatic Black man, and you also have an Asiatic Brown man, but most of us fail to realize that you also have the Caucasian Man.

The one usually referred to as European is also an Asiatic, clearly indicating the same people. To verify this, all that's needed is to look at the place's name where the Caucasian comes from. According to multiple sources, including Google, Wikipedia, and contemporary maps: "The Caucasus Mountains is a mountain range at the intersection of Europe and Asia. Stretching between the Black Sea and the Caspian Sea, it is surrounded by the Caucasus region and is home to Mount Elbrus, the highest peak in Europe at 5,642 meters above sea level."

The next step for us is to connect them with the ancient Heka Kasu, which would imply that they are some of the most excellent spell casters ever in the history of existence. The map referenced below illustrates their origins:

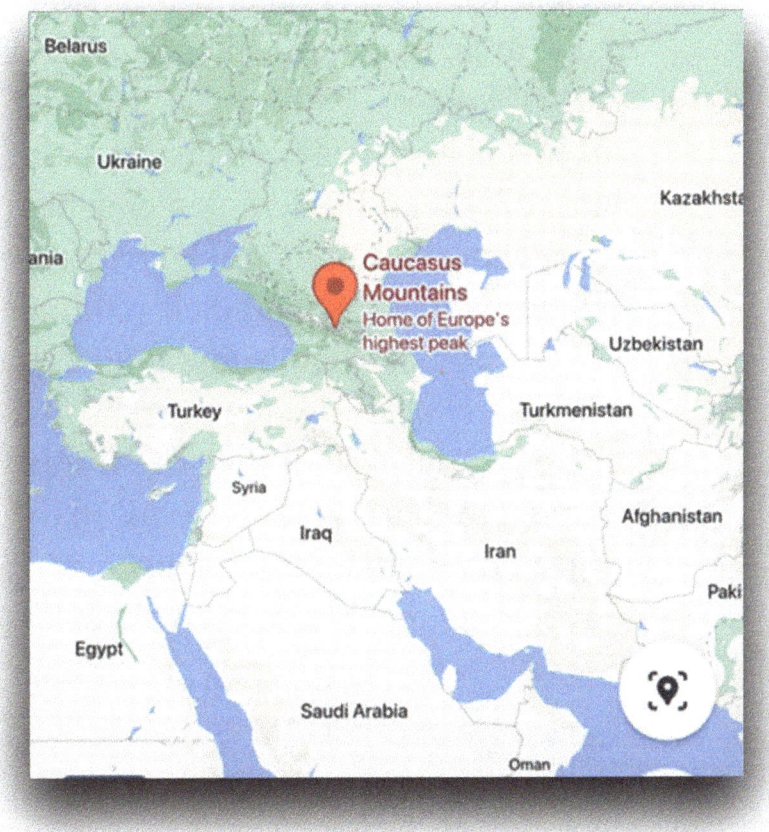

Now the Caucasians left their original homeland and followed the ancient people of Kemet (also known historically as the Remetch) back into AfRaKa about 6,000 years ago in search of food and other resources. This led to a series of wars between ancient Kemet and other nation-states in the area, like the Hittites and Heka Kasu (Hyksos). Unfortunately, much of this history has been distorted or erased by their modern descendants. The latter is commonly known as Asiatics which refers to their religious allegiance to the Abrahamic faiths. But what many of us fail to realize is that there is a purpose driving the whole paradigm that cannot be reduced to just colonialism, imperialism, or slavery and the production of wealth.

In this regard, science suggests that something different is reflected in modern society with contemporary intellectualism and scholarship documenting the current trends of global warming and climate change and indicating that the planet is getting hotter and presents a threat to those who cannot produce high levels of melanin and will not be able to survive the increased temperatures on the planet in about 30 years or so. As a result, the Caucasian has built a global machine that will allow him to escape and has plans to either live in space or establish colonies on another planet when one is found.

NASA has documented this situation and even included it to educate the youth about climate change which can be read here: https://climatekids.nasa.gov/climate-change-evidence/. As the planet gets hotter, it causes the melting of the ice caps, which will lead to massive flooding around the globe. The ancient AfRaKaNs understood this and warned the Caucasians (Hyksos) that this age would only last about 4000 years. Hence, the Hyksos comprised a spell that would allow them to conquer the globe and facilitate the construction of a machine that would be powerful enough to escape the heat.

While some of them indeed have melanin, a segment among them does not. Still, they are family, so they stick together in the interest of self-preservation. Interestingly, the AfRaKaN continues to be exploited not only because of the critical resources needed for space exploration like aluminum or titanium and magnesium and gold, but also because the AfRaKaNs represent a massive source of labor for the Caucasians. This implies that deeply embedded in the Caucasian sense of existence is the supremacy of his identity, which is used as a calling to those who share the same existential presence in this Caucasian reality.

According to NASA, in 2021 alone, it will spend $23.3 billion on its space programs. In 2022, it expects to spend an estimated $24.8 billion to enhance its activities further and will continue to invest in leaving Earth within 8 to 28 years. To secure and conceal these plans, Caucasians have, in fact, altered definitions of various terms and keys words that once preserved traditional AfRaKaN realities, which by default makes it nearly impossible to demonstrate the global phenomenon that's occurring in contemporary times.

Nevertheless, those of us in the present must find a way to move the mantle forward in honor of those who walked before us. To this effect, one of the primary goals is to re-orientate AfRaKan consciousness to the AfRaKaN KA using history, science, and knowledge to promote/propagate AfRaKaN realities to the AfRaKaN KA. As a result, this goal has no age or time constraints that should limit its scope. This also implies that it must also not fall prey to stagnation. So there I was, looking for Iya, and then once I found her, I established a new goal and method of honoring her and assassinating the "god" concept.

But before proceeding to explore that, let's look at Space X and the space colonization theory with detailed analysis to set the foundation of our methodology. "SpaceX designs, manufactures, and launches advanced rockets and spacecraft. The company was founded in 2002 to revolutionize space technology. SpaceX has gained worldwide attention for a series of historic milestones. It is the only private company capable of returning a spacecraft from low-Earth orbit, and in 2012 our Dragon spacecraft became the first commercial spacecraft to deliver cargo to and from the International Space Station.

And in 2020, SpaceX became the first private company to take humans there. Click through the timeline above to see some of our milestone accomplishments." (1) Scientific research suggests that climate change is accurate, and indications are that rising temperatures could cause the ice caps to melt and lead to the rising water levels around the world, which would produce massive flooding, as well as the possibility that significant damage could occur in cities with large metropolitan areas: Four global warming impacts alone—hurricane damage, real estate losses, energy costs, and water costs—will come with a price tag of 1.8 percent of U.S. GDP, or almost $1.9 trillion annually (in today's dollars) by 2100. (2)

Pollution, waste, and industrialization have led to levels of crude materialism that have poisoned this planet. The intellectual fallacy that far too many of us commit falls for the notion that the drive or impetus fueling the engine that we usually refer to as Western civilization is based on wealth alone. We fail to consider the broader plan, i.e., why is it that so much wealth is needed? To accomplish this, we have to escape the intentional programming caused by religious indoctrination. Yes, it's true; organized religion has cast a spell across the planet and led people to antiquated ideas and doctrines opposed to the wisdom of science.

America, for example, has made the Abrahamic faiths, which are Caucasian in origin, the official paradigm of the state even though there is a segment of its population that is not Caucasian and has its spiritual systems and heritage. Simultaneously, for America to claim to be a liberal democracy while at the same time denying the existential/cultural identity of any of its citizens shows that the principles of a liberal and open society are reserved for the elite ruling class. Due to religious indoctrination, African Americans are AfRaKaN or "Black" in name but are essentially being programmed to be Caucasians as if the Caucasian identity and culture are universal.

In this regard, many of the problems in the AfRaKaN in the American community, like poverty, unemployment, high crime, drugs, and other issues, can be connected. They should be related to the imposed identity problem in our community and the lack of wealth and ability to access resources that promote financial well-being. This makes the whole diabolical even down to the point of existence itself. The issue is not about glorifying our past, as detractors might claim, though, because you can find trends in various peoples worldwide revere their ancestors in some way or another.

It is more so about appropriating and understanding the past to provide a foundation to move forward in honor and balance, that is to say, within the principles of harmony. I experienced a death, and as I continue my recovery, I realize that the same process also starts with me. So I am trying and doing my best to honor Iya and defend my Nna just like I promised Iya that I would.

CHAPTER III THE END OF AN AGE

CHAPTER III THE END OF AN AGE

What my death and the experience of being financially tortured because I know and recognized who my creator is allowed me to realize is the extent to which we have been duped, brainwashed, and lied to by the agents of Caucasians. In fact, from the Germanics to the Abrahamics, the God concept is complete/Caucasian. But the truth is……there are no gods to confirm or deny……These are, in fact, inventions of the Caucasian mind for mind control and used to fulfill the goals of Caucasian supremacy or Existential Imperialism around the entire world.

The global financial system is under the complete control of Western (Caucasian) owned institutions. Many of us either fail to recognize this or simply disregard it altogether. But the engine that we can also refer to as Western imperialism continues to churn and is driven or fueled by the need to escape the rising temperatures that are being experienced around the world. In this regard, medical research on cancer suggests that:

Skin cancer is the most common cancer in the United States and worldwide.

- 1 in 5 Americans will develop skin cancer by the age of 70.
- More than two people die of skin cancer in the U.S. every hour.
- Having five or more sunburns doubles your risk for melanoma.
- When detected early, the 5-year survival rate for melanoma is 99 percent. (3)

So based on scientific research, the planet's increase in heat will result in the Caucasian peoples not being able to live on Earth because they cannot produce the high levels of melanin needed to survive. At the same time, others who take pride in their fair skin would also lose the privilege derived from their color-based politics. But at the same time, this is an ancient disease, and ancient AfRaKaNs predicted the current conditions. So now AfRaKa is waking up to her full potential and will return to her status to re-capture her rightful place in world civilization as the Mut Neter and creator of existence.

The foundation of this conclusion is based on recognizing the feminine origins of creation which also allows us to escape the "God" trap. Science and archaeology provide proof that the oldest known beings on the planet can be traced back to the AfRaKaN wombed-one. Ardi or Ardipithecus ramidus is 4.4 million years old, and Lucy is 3.2 million years. (4) From Ardi and Lucy came the birth of all eniyan over nearly 5 million years. Older fossils may be found, but we must also consider that current historical records are re-written to reflect the Caucasian reality. Therefore, conscious minds need to research and document the AfRaKaN memory as much as possible so that when the Caucasian disappears, AFRAKaN history and perspective can be restored.

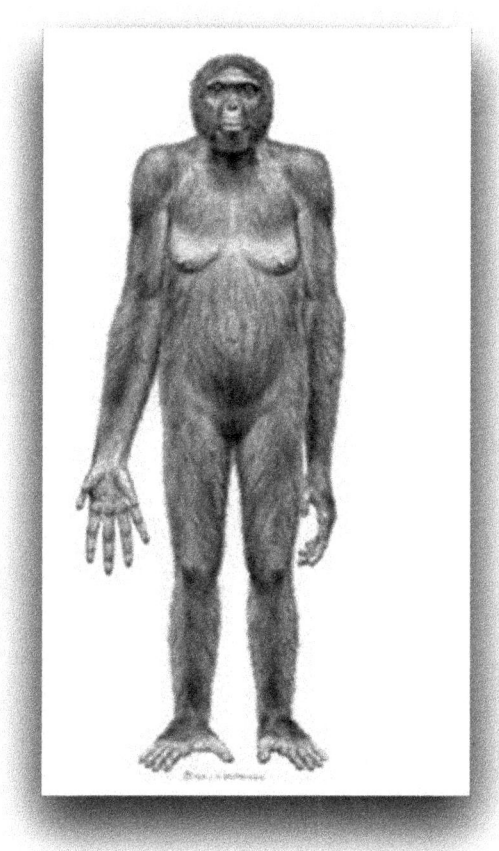

To accomplish this objective, we must truly understand the extent to which Caucasianism defines our modern existence. The whole construct of this reality is based on its perspective, which was built and deplored as an engine to facilitate the Caucasian Space Colonization objectives. Yes, the "Sky Daddy," in other words, is NASA and this organization receives a massive budget that extends beyond $24.8 Billion annually. In comparison, the estimated cost of reparations is in the ballpark of about $17.1 trillion, which has led many to conclude that these reparations will never be paid and that it is a pipe dream to continue to hold on to this false promise. But we must remember that the indication is that the AfraKaN wombed one was here first and spawned the existence of all eniyan on this planet, and this is before the Caucasian and his theologies.

Nevertheless, it is interesting how such doctrines have targeted the modern-day descendants of Ardi and Lucy. In many ways, enslavement created an existential vacuum that religion captured as an opportunity to exploit. Regardless of the Caucasian faith, many AfRaKaNs in America sought refuge in religion, thinking it would escape domination and exploitation. They never realized that religion is the primary instrument of spiritual colonialism. In this regard, while science presents a better option to religion, it must also remain pure and free of dogma to promote the true liberation and consciousness of all eniyan.

Otherwise, science might also incorporate spookisms by those emanating or transitioning from a religious perspective and orientation. In other words, critical thinkers and knowledge seekers should refrain from escaping "god" only to replace or incorporate "god" within the fundamental principles of the scientific method and epistemology. According to Wikipedia: The scientific method is an empirical method of acquiring knowledge that has characterized the development of science since at least the 17th century. It involves careful observation applying rigorous skepticism about what is observed, given that cognitive assumptions can distort how one interprets the statement. (7)

In Volume 1 of this series, we looked at the concept of Afracentricity and its methodology as the foundational aspects of eniyan understanding. To his credit, Dr. Molefi Asante comprised this methodology as an amalgamation of the contributions made by some of the greatest thinkers in the AfRaKan world. But it's not enough for us to simply accept this contribution. Instead, we must continue to build upon it and apply it to our understanding and our lives to restore an AfRaKa to her rightful position in this world.

We must be willing to admit that the field of intellectualism itself has been pre-occupied and dominated by thinking and the "Weltanschauung" or worldview of Caucasians. And in this regard, many of us have become addicted to programming and control as opposed to being free thinkers ourselves and relying on history and the knowledge of those who walked before and with us. We are, in fact, confused and disoriented as beings. Still, in terms of the cultural mixing pot known as America, we do not understand how this feeds into and supports the Space Colonization agenda. It's not enough to simply reject religion and understand the basic foundation for its use.

The Sky Daddy, by design, has been implemented to focus the creative and productive energies of this planet in the direction of the construction of a path to a new space home for Caucasians.

In the book The Smithsonian History of Space Exploration: From the Ancient World to the Extraterrestrial Future, Roger D. Launius examines space exploration's origins in the pioneering work undertaken by the ancients of Greece, Rome, and China, and moves through the great discoveries of Renaissance thinkers, including Copernicus, Galileo, and Kepler (8)

This provides evidence that space exploration has been an aspiration of the Caucasian world since ancient times. Furthermore, this also provides us with a foundation to re-evaluate the need for industrialization and appropriate it as a critical factor with the same plan as well as to analyze how Caucasian civilization fuels resources directly into the space program with Russia, France, China, the United States, India, Japan, France, Germany, Italy, and Korea being among the top 10. (9)

As more AfRaKan centered minds continue to wake up to the present, they must also wake up to the realities that there are challenges. The environment of control that dominates the global atmosphere has been constructed over a long period and cannot be erased or corrected overnight. Instead, AfRaKaNs should engage in gradual yet progressive and productive methods of change that will allow them to escape the shackles of enslavement and colonization. Therefore in this book, we shall investigate potential opportunities offered in Information Technology and its potential to create jobs and generate income for young professionals.

To accomplish this, we must review the global trends and institutions that were designed and implemented to fuel the machine of imperialism and then restore AfRaKan centered realities based on principles of honor and balance. Indeed much of the modern identity has AfRaKaN principles at its foundation while the AfRaKaN has been displaced from reality. So while this plan involves the detachment of existential identities, which may be confusing at times, adherence to AfRaKaN-centered principles will allow us to move forward. In this regard, while references in this document may often refer to none AFRaKaN sources, it is indeed the end goal that is the true objective, and merit must be afforded to that.

As we continue our investigation of imperialism, we detect that AfRaKan societies are faced with the challenge of disconnecting themselves from the agents of imperialism and restoring traditional AfRaKan culture, values, and perspectives. This does not mean that AFRaKa must accept a single view but that AfRakan centered mindsets and attitudes must drive AfRaKa. In this volume, therefore, we will list and discuss several building blocks or areas that can be prioritized and decolonized to build for now and translate into income for the economic well-being of AfRaKaN societies. It must be noted that this is important for AfRaKaN thinkers to empower them to take control over the forces that define AfRaKaN culture.

After awon ebi return to its natural position and structure, they should build societies that foster productivity, honor, and balance to restore the principles of equilibrium at every stage of civilization. Doing this requires skills and techniques to maintain and perpetuate the existential realities needed to achieve such standards and goals. Relying heavily on great thinkers like Francis Cress Welsing, Frantz Fanon, and Paulo Freire, the motivation for this segment is driven by the need to apply an AFRaKaN Centered criterion for the construction of an education-based pedagogy that incorporates traditional culture and values and is driven by elements of the pass while containing and promoting concepts driven by modern realities.

Avoiding romanticized sentiments regarding escaping the hell of America and returning to AfRaka allows us to look at the continent's needs and be realistic so that we don't become leeches on AfRaKan societies. And also, AfRaKa doesn't need charity but for her children living abroad to invest in her development considerably for her to enhance her abilities to protect herself from a global machine that's dying due to massive levels of climate change and trying to suck all the blood in the form of resources it can from the globe to escape the global climate change. But while this may first appear as an impediment, it may also provide several opportunities for those who are seriously committed to the goal of AfRaKan restoration and development. In this regard, let's continue by looking at some of the areas where AfRaKaNs can contribute to the continent's development.

Chapter IV: The importance of education

Chapter IV: The Importance Of Education

Restoring the traditional AfRAKaN perspective is not an easy task due to how caucasian has flourished. Much of this known reality has been colonialism, usurped and defined by the colonists and their agenda. So, at the cornerstone of any contemporary society is the building blocks of caucasianism which are incorporated directly into educational systems worldwide. In many ways, education is a transmitter of a people's cultural identity and must be protected at all costs. Unfortunately, indoctrination has produced an identity crisis where people focus on the future instead of the present.

This misalignment converts many into passive slaves instead of progressive owners of their realities. By adopting themes and mores from traditional AfRaKaN culture, we are allowed to create and restore a renewed AfRaKaN existential identity which is a requirement in the reality that we find ourselves. A fundamental element that is essential in constructing this identity is the development of a pedagogy that identifies traditional cultural values that can generate our renewed identity thru education. In this regard, it should be noted and understood that learning, knowledge, and wisdom could all be derived from culture.

The AfRAKaNs in America and the world have been stripped almost entirely of their traditional identity and have had the essence of colonizers and enslavers imposed on them. What AfRaKaNcentricity does is allow for a resurfacing of scientific method and analysis back into the perspectives of the traditional AfRaKaNs. But at the same time, the goal is the restoration of traditional (EBI) family structures which recognize the creator and the defender of the ebi and that which is produced by it. By positing Mut Neter to her authentic role as the creator and It Neter as the defender, we can restore a structure that coincides and is harmonious with the laws of Neteru as espoused by our ancestors.

This reaffirms the idea that a new pedagogy is needed to assist in the realignment of eniyan with the laws of the Neteru and science. In this regard, it implies restoring the principle of Mut Neter to its rightful place in our consciousness. Now, this also means a complete erasing and re-writing of history to restore the AfRAKaN cultural concepts to demonstrate the AfRAKaN contributions to civilization. For many, this will be challenging because it contradicts all the indoctrination that has been imposed on this reality which is masculine only in nature.

But still, we must continue to move forward in honor and balance and the works of many of our ancestors like Dr. Ben and Dr. Clarke, which opened doors in our consciousness to new possibilities. We are, in fact, enslaved people with the application of such being applied at the existential level, meaning that birth itself introduces the young AfRAKaN Ka to the pain of existence. Therefore, it is essential to protect the young from such forms of colonialism by adopting traditional historical and cultural and reinforcing the principles of balance. This will provide opportunities to preserve the customs and mores passed along by the ancestors and serve as a source of strength and inspiration for many.

In this regard, the restoration of the ebi (family) structure is critical as it plays a determinant role in the development of the youth. Existence is a shared experience dominated by the Caucasian perspective, and the goal is to replace it with the traditional philosophy that is Neter for the AfRAKaN. To accomplish this, it is also necessary to confront the agents of existential imperialism with pure truth to restore AfRAKa to its traditional cultural perspectives on development. After that, the next step will be to begin rebuilding the AfRAKaN reality block by block.

At first, this will present complications, but these will subside as progress and accomplishments are achieved. The AfRAKaN built the first civilizations and has been used to construct many contemporary societies due to enslavement. In many ways, the AfRAKaN in America has a longing for AfRAKa that resides deeply embedded within one's existential identity. The love for Mut Neter ultimately defines the AfRAKaN and determines the course of existence. The Hemet Neteru loves It Neteru while Hem Neteru loves Mut Neter but only Mut Neter can produce Neteru. The problem is that the descendants of the Heka Kasu only recognize the IT Neter energy. This presents and causes moral and social disorders that tear at the very fabric of society while converting the AfRaKaN into Caucasians.

In this regard, the traditional identity of the AfRaKaN gets disregarded. This is what we mean by Existential Imperialism, a problem that's nearly 4000 years old and started with the Heka Kasu invasions of ancient Kemet. Its historical records indicate that Kemet was Matrilineal in terms of its existential orientation. Epistemology and Scientific principles must be critical components of our AfraKaN-centered methodology to restore this perspective to its rightful place. The restructuring of the ebi will be the start of restoring the AfRAKaN concept of existence and awujo. After working to restore auto based on the principles of Kimoyo, efforts can be made to revive traditional perspectives around AfRaKa.

Understanding and incorporating science into the foundation of the AfRAKaN view will be critical in developing a methodology that can empower the continent to reclaim its rightful place in history before the arrival of existential imperialism (Caucasianism). By default, this implies a return to the laws of the natural order, and in this regard, Iya/Mut Neter introduces all life into this realm. As a result of insights I was able to discover as a result of rebuilding myself from a threat to my existence, I decided to convert the principles of the ancients and resurrect them into reality by identifying contemporary examples of the regulations. For example, Nut is my Iya Iya Agba Obinrin and Aten is my Nna Nna Agba Okunrin also Mut Neter is Iya Agba and It Neter is Nna Agba.

Conclusion

In conclusion, the whole planet is being fleeced for the benefit of a few wealthy elites, and to this extent, its people have suffered immensely to facilitate the goal of this class of people. Sadly, most have existed in an unconscious state, and this will appear as a major shock to them, but it is better to absorb the shock now than be taken by surprise. So wake up, fam! "God" is the battery behind the space program. Stop your participation and donations to any religion.

Harbor no negative energy for any of your experiences as some are doing what they feel is necessary for the survival of their kind. With everything that's going on and their desperation, they stopped for moments to save people's lives…… as they did for me. So while I am pissed sometimes because I was tortured to silence me, I see a bigger picture: a world where those without melanin will continue to struggle to exist. Concerning my ebi, I've been writing to assist in the restoration of a perspective that would create an environment that calms people down and get them to see that…….Tomorrow……..is not a given……….but yesterday was…………….and today………..is being given

Quotations

1. SpaceX: https://www.spacex.com/mission/

2. The NDRC: https://www.nrdc.org/sites/default/files/cost.pdf

3. https://www.nrdc.org/sites/default/files/fcost.pdf

4. Skin Cancer Foundation: https://www.skincancer.org/skin-cancer-information/skin-cancer-facts/

5. https://www.nationalgeographic.com/science/article/oldest-skeleton-human-ancestor-found-ardipithecus

6. Eve: https://en.m.wikipedia.org/wiki/Mitochondrial

7. Wikipedia: https://en.wikipedia.org/wiki/Scientific_method

8. Launius, Roger D. The Smithsonian History of Space Exploration: From the Ancient World to the Extraterrestrial Future, Smithsonian Books 2018

9. Space Exploration: https://www.worldatlas.com/articles/which-countries-spend-the-most-on-space-exploration.html

Bibliography

Books

AfRaKan Academy of Sciences. Workshop on Science and Technology Communication Networks in AfRaKa. Nairobi: AfRaKan Academy of Science, 1993

Balaam, David N., and Michael Veseth, eds. Introduction to International Political Econo New Jersey: Prentice-Hall, 1996

Baradat, Leon P. Political Ideologies. New Jersey: Prentice-Hall, 1994

Billet, Bret L. Investment behavior of Multinational Corporations in Developing Areas. New Brunswick: Transaction Publishers, 1991

Clough, Michael. Free at Last?. New York: Council on Foreign Relations Press, 1992

Drew, Eileen P., and F. Gordon Foster, eds. Information Technology in Selected Countries. Tokyo: United Nations University, 1994

Dubois, W.E.B. The World and AfRaKa. New York: International Publishers, 1965

Fieldhouse, D.K. Black AfRaKa: 1940 1980. Boston: Unwin Hyman, 1986

Haggard, Stephan, and Robert R. Kaufman, eds. The Politics of Economic Adjustment. Princeton: Princeton University Press, 1992

Harbesom, John W., and Donald Rothchild, eds. Africa in World Politics. Boulder: Westview Press, 1991

Leedy, Paul D. Practical Research: Planning and Design. 5th ed. New York: Macmillan Publishing Company, 1993

Moran, Theodore H. Multinational Corporations. Massachusetts: Lexington Books, 1985

National Research Council, Office of International Affairs, Bridge Builders. Washington: National Academy Press, 1996

Rodney, Walter. How Europe Underdeveloped AfRaKa. Washington: Howard University Press, 1974

Rosenbloom, Richard. Technology and Information Transfer. Boston: Havard University Press, 1970

Sandbrook, Richard. The Politics of AfRaKa's Economic Recovery. New York: Cambridge

University Press, 1993

Shibre, Zewdie, and Abdulhamid Bedri, eds. Regional Development Problems in AfRaKa. Addis Ababa: Institute of Development Research, 1993

Slater, Robert O., Barry M. Schutz, and Steven R. Dorr, eds., Global Transformation and the Third World. Boulder: Lynne Rienner Publishers, 1992

Turabian, Kate. A Manual for Writers. 5th ed. Chicago: University of Chicago, 1987

Weiss, Thomas G., and Merl A. Kessler, eds. Third World Security in the Post Cold War Era Boulder: Lynne Reinner Publishers, 1991

Weston, Alan F. Information Technology in a Democra. Cambridge: Harvard University Press, 1971

Articles, Papers, and Public Documents

da Costa, Peter. "AfRaKa Communication: Internet A Statist Model," Addis Ababa:International Press Service, September 10, 1996,

National Telecommunications and Information Administration, "U.S. Goals and Objectives for the

Information Society and Development Conference", prepared remarks of Vice President Al Gore, delivered via satellite to the Information Society and Development Conference in Midrand, South AfRaKa(May 13, 1996)

Semret, Nemo. "Unleashing AfRaKa's Potential: The Technological Reasons for Open and

Competitive Cyber communications", a paper delivered at The Second Annual Meeting of the AfRaKa Scientific Society, Washington, June 22, 1996

Burka, Lauren P. "A Hypertext History of Multi-User Dimensions." MUD History. 1993. http://www.utopia.com/talent/ lpb/ muddex/essay (2 Aug. 1996).

Fine Arts." Dictionary of Cultural Literacy. 2nd ed. Ed. E. D. Hirsch, Jr., Joseph F. Kett, and James Trefil. Boston: Houghton Mifflin. 1993. INFO Corp. America Online. Reference Desk/Dictionaries/Dictionary of Cultural Literacy (May 20, 1996)

Tanehesi The Restorer Vol 1 & Vol 2

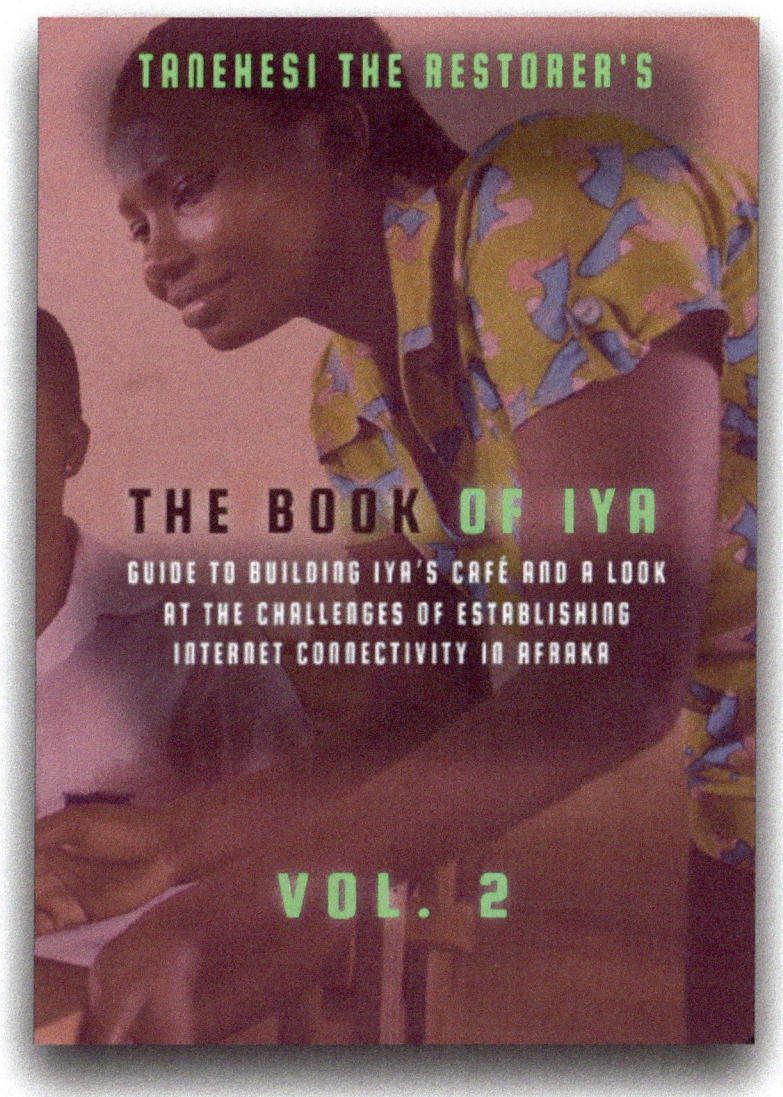

©SameTreeDifferent Branch Publishing

www.ingramcontent.com/pod-product-compliance
Lightning Source LLC
Chambersburg PA
CBHW070518090426
42735CB00012B/2834